Peter Philpott

Also by Peter Philpott:

The Bishop Stortford Variations (Great Works Editions, 1976)
What Was Shown (Ferry Press, London, 1980)
Some Action Upon The World (Grosseteste, Leeds, 1982)

TEXTUAL POSSESSIONS

Three Sequences by

Peter Philpott

> Dammit these words are making faces
> At me again. I hope the faces
> They make at you have more love.
>
>> WS Graham,
>> from "Implements in Their Places"
>> *New Collected Poems*

First published in the United Kingdom in 2004 by
Shearsman Books
58 Velwell Road
Exeter EX4 4LD

http://www.shearsman.com/

ISBN 0-907562-53-1

Copyright © Peter Philpott 2003, 2004.
The right of Peter Philpott to be identified as the author of this work has been asserted by him in accordance with the Copyrights, Designs and Patents Act of 1988. All rights reserved. No part of this publication may be reproduced, stored in a retrieval system, transmitted in any form or by any means, electronic, mechanical, photocopying, recording or otherwise, without the prior permission of the publisher.

Front cover photograph of Minehead Beach by the author, copyright © Peter Philpott, 2004. Rear cover photograph of the author by Minna Kantonen, copyright © Minna Kantonen, 2004.

Acknowledgements

Some of these texts originally appeared in *Angel Exhaust*, *Tears in the Fence*, and on www.greatworks.org.uk

CONTENTS

In the Present Historic Sense
A Serial Poem of the West   7

An Encounter Upon the Beach at Minehead
With the Prince of This World   67

On Being Voiced: High Steps Breeding
(a Broadcast of Radio Alterity)   97

IN THE PRESENT HISTORIC TENSE
A Serial Poem of the West

Alcmaeon says that men die because they cannot attach the beginning to the end – a clever saying if you take it to have been meant loosely and do not try to make it precise.

> (pseudo-Aristotle, Problem 916933-37,
> from ed. Jonathan Barnes,
> *Early Greek Philosophy* [Penguin, 1987])

I OF THE WEST

1

On the grey beach
Men hammer madly at
The talismans of a lost past
Unknown but believed in
Compulsively shattering
The secret's not released
But broken.

Purchase and achievement spread it
That perfect find repeated
As the miracle of commodity
Swopping it if lucky
Colour postcards of the stars
The piledriver hammering
Red rusty walls
Against a glass-green sea
Bright under the breakwater
Sucking and pulling stones
Until the town and all the people
Lost as the dinosaurs and the ammonites
No one wants to find us

Our secret will be safe
Unbroken inside concrete boulders
Red soft pebbles of bricks
Old worn glass and slivers of plastic
Spreading out and losing themselves
Against the grey black sagging cliffs

2

In the town of the old men
Quiet and friendliness
Grow in little gardens
Bright flowers around the lawns
Red bean-flowers climbing at the back
The soft fruit murmuring to itself
Under a flawless eggshell sky.

This whole thing hurts:
It pushes in, soft
Furnishing tucks caught and pinned
With great care, love and neatness.
The pins are those
That murder saints and insects
Silently, quietly and like a friend
Under this flawless soft blue sky.

It hurts because it is inevitable
Irresistible, slow and unwanted
The whole body tumorous, or
Swathed in black bugs, while tea
Cups clatter and soft voices reminisce
In rooms pumped out of air.
The sky is still blue.

In the town of the old men
The old dogs, old food, old houses
Old words drift like aphids
Sparkling in perpetual sunlight
And settling, now welcomed
Into their places, quiet
Friendly and wanted at last.

3

And at this place
Flocks of jackdaws
Like a plague

Telling us messages
Over and over
Like the waves

"You can't win
You will get old
Die like everyone else"

These wise birds
Live everywhere here
Like the people

The town and
The bare rocky valleys
Like gorges, dead lakes

Where the river fell out
It dried
Piled like rock

Ruins and legends
All false, impossible
Like we knew

What the birds tell us
Eyes black beads in white
Like automata

Or like some
Wisdom burst out
A dreadful warning

Black bodies flying
Into night, sky
And sea

4

The familiar green world
Beyond the hill opening
Into heaviness, old lawrentian words
Sprouting up and pushing
Fecund, heavy and burgeoning:

The familiar green world
Beyond the one we know
Tread upon but opening
Behind it
Here, now

The familiar green world
Beyond
A child's picture
Of the wild world
Opening out around

The familiar green world beyond
Any one spot
Only comings into growth
And dying in a dance
Opening to this

Familiar green world
Beyond

5

The bus promised Hardy country
Slow and dirty, faintly melancholy
With the abandoned air of all public things

Distant views across also possible
Drifts of time and vapour allowing
But never a visit:

The buses stopped before the heights
And you were lost in a dirty town
Returning always to the familiar haunts

The nearer edge is the safer
Can't undo what is cut, not cut except
Nightmare fantasies.

Going back to the familiar green world
Beyond the familiar green places
That aren't the world but a world

Haphazard and torn, unconvincing
And boring as posters in buses
With the abandoned air of all public things

6

The road runs between water
To the horizons grey reflective skies
Like nature's way: something vast

Impersonal and beautiful, regular
Predictable as language, reflective
Meaning too that underneath

It's not the sky but muddy grass
Punctuated by consonants
We all know this

But love the infinite sheens of surfaces
All you need for reflection
Can't stop it or understand

Meaning like water
Doesn't go away
But slowly returns

Can't keep it out
Stretching
To either horizon

7

We inhabit old films
Black and white westerns glimpsed over the sundays
Family entertainment
The latest british film
Patriotic, stiff and half humorous at least
Deprecating fatally itself and us

Everything switches from under to overplay
Like mad relatives
Threatening impossible people Dad works for
Teachers seen out of school
Like travesties of the real people they are
Threatening or helpful
We also inhabit

And shops that don't exist
Grocers making up orders
Drapers and ironmongers
Quiet respectable places
Where you were known and
Everyone knows you as the bell
Rings, a real bell

Like the sound of the fire engine
Everyone gets out to watch
The double show:
Getting to it
And then it rushes off clanging
But it won't come back
Stuck in the memory

A faded land
We all really inhabit
Make it our own
It gets to know us and to love us
Each detail
Unless lost or broken
Slowly reappearing
Sharpens

8

Parts hazy or insecure
What is a screen memory
And how different from what you are told
Was so?

Imagine a field flooded and iced
No action as dangerous as skating
But the pleasures of walking and breaking

The ice bubbled, cracked and refrozen
Filthy with mud and grasses
Sheets of it covering the fields
Is this

Real or a trick? The ice
Fractures, cold dark fluid under
Welling up and recovering.
It freezes

Then vanishes
The next day.

9

The wind in the willows
Sliding in from the north
Invariably painful, cold

Playing among ruins
Abandoned refuges
Little hills above the floods

A slight natural advantage
Insufficient to stop
The wind or people

Abandoned towers
Settlement traces and hearths
Swept over just by the wind

Moving the withies
Cold enough to bring pain
Cut to the bone

Abandoned stones
Broken beams and engines
Looking out

Over a conquered country
No reason to stay
The places were left

For the floods and the wind
And the slow abandoned decay
Twisting structures like memories

Blown about like
A field of withies
Under the wind.

II MEMORIES OF THE FUTURE

1

A band on what?
Someone left, then
Continuity demands
A repeat

You breathe? Yes
Denise Riley and Cole
Ridge know this, go
Ing on very abrupt
Vertiginous
That's liable to make you chuck up
Or even yourself down
Somewhere pretty horrible
An epileptic pull
Out of the slightly normal rhythms
That stop us noticing

Oh, formalism
A strange hope
That there are
Only words
Sourced and sluiced
Run over rapids
Provide some kind of ground
Cropping up beneath

Never abandoned
Dwelt on by ghosts and delusions of being
Poor human presences
Gibbering through our withies
A band of unbanal
Memories and pains

2

Why not look at art?
Why not collect up
The sagging tissues? Why
Not return to milk bottles
Braces and real tea?
Use it to settle the dust.
It is virtually certain reality
Operates through batches and memory-makers
It is virtually certain human love
Will swim through such viscid media
Seeking upriver for its birth
And if fooled
Will end

It is virtually certain
Questions will end: each one
Tested and proved, stamped on in advance
Why not just stop?

This whole business went on
Far too long
Lost a lot of words
Attrited, degraded, leached out
A taluslike slope creeping
Intermittently downwards into a broad
River of stones: moving
Into dust and wind

At the end
The machines broke
The art laughed
The flesh continued
With all the attendant emotions
Hiding and flying
Like a shoal of small, playful fish

3

Late (always) and in pain
Mild pain: stumped and wintry
Abandoned in a waste of grass

4

Stars are pilot lights
Everything changes into what it is:
At once and with
Suspension of time, belief and the normal clear gel
In between us and
Anything else just goes in
One clear flash:

The darkness is a thin liquid
Warm and sexual
Fetching both male and female
Object and being together

You light the gas
Put on the kettle
Wait for it to boil
Hiss
Pour a little, empty
Add tea and pour
Wait while it steeps
Then pour it
With absolute grace
Into a cup or bowl
Adding whatever else you fancy

While you do this
The poem already fades and washes off
And another one
You write
Sipping the tea

It is a better poem.

5

Small creatures also live in this place
Their bodies glowing jewels that unlike us
Are not just smelling of the decay of our flesh
Which falls from us in strips and tatters
Or moistened by mucus swells blindly. They
Look at us with hatred, amazement and occasional love
Also fear, for they know how desperate and unpredictable
We can be when we realise who
And what we are now.

6 New Year Poem

Like the children stuck
In some colossal stupid game
Blindly on into the night
Rushing out and in:
                            it's
Three o'clock, it's nearly midnight
And I am 43 or 4
Here. Why?

Lucid interrogations of language
Can't help any more than personal expression, or
Ideological construct or process
Acting against what set it up.

Suddenly it is
Cold rain, responsibility and the return
Of the bad dreams
The ones of falling

This is where you pause in falling
And realise
Acceleration is what is constant
And what that means
How short
At the end of life
To look back on it all
As there was nothing
There but an unfinished game
A few chalk marks and bits
Like outgrown clothes
Worn out bodies
Suddenly
Come round faster
Again

7

Every loss scars
After some point
Not outgrowing this
But letting fall
Or be fallen
The whole thing
Dropped at the end

8

Is the status of pronouns
Less interesting than clouds and clarity
Winter evenings a form of discourse
Totally hegemonic but also ineffectual:
All that red stain
Alters nothing, profusely
Conservative it happens again
And again uncaring
And blind as words
Themselves?

9

What if the poem's hereditary
Written each time the same
Just a different dress or expression
The body of words identical and pushed out
From some little tricks of the cells?

10

It's how not
Adequate fantasy is
Under a regime
Of total postponement
Negative financing, debt
To time increasing
More and more
Unable to do
When the collapse
Reaches just here
The point stops:
A still voice
In that pause:
That last chance
Before the dive
Diving down into
Into the blackness
Necessity breaking over
Like heavy surf
Dark rocks, a
Backswell, a slap
Against the stone
The dive down
Again into fantasy
Knowing it inadequate
Knowing its destination
Reaching out, reaching out
Shortcircuiting imagination
With detritus, junk
Ground up, not
Adequate, what happens
Will be worse

III ROTE

1

Continuity demands a repeat
That idea of talisman holding it all
While you break it, break it

It is only certain rhythms
Folding into us
Then catching
Abrading the filmstock all this
Town, sea, writing and the whole
Nothing can hold it or find
Everything snapped into blackness
And a dead repeated noise
Hammer at a stone
To get inside

Wearing down
Building up
Faith in orogenesis and drift
Those structures alone uncommodified
Pure beautiful forms
Cropping up like perfect pebbles in the streambed
The red ones
Are us

Never abandoned
Dwelt on by ghosts and delusions
Poor human presences
Waiting frantic
For the rock to split

2

As people decay art grows
Then drops. The sky
Not basically altering
Is always blue, high, clear
A transparent thin medium
Etching grain and dust
Fascination stops

It is a pretence
Virtually certain
A trick of the light
Suspiciously flawless

The blue haze of unknowing
Just different from purity, pain
Perfection: arising through time
Vastly slow and irregular
Anomalous and intermittent

Eventually drifting everywhere
Like aphids sparkling in the air as perpetual sunshine
Or fish
Small dark minnow darting
A swift moving cloud
Poised in their fluid
Clear and everywhere.

3

Late, always
And in pain
Abandoned in a waste of grass

Meaning
Rolling through it
As if

Articulate
Or even true
Nothing survives

Lives separate
Inescapable
Garrulous birds

Dotting the grass in the town
The bare rocks where it ends
Slips down into the sea

That's also uncertain
As prophecy
Cries of birds

What they tell us
Blind and automatic
Black and white

Affect nothing here
Wisdom escaped
Warned

Flown at night
Into the dark glowing sky
And what lies beyond

4

Beyond colour, colour
Specific and qualitied
Existing absolute as stars
As domestic paraphernalia of lights, switches
Jolting us through our days
And beyond into the night

Into a familiar world
Bathed in a clear fluid
Where flying becomes like swimming
Like thinking, like fucking
Like in that myth of presence
Always beyond

Beyond our acts
And in them: pouring
An arc of glittering water
In the morning, in the evening
Sitting in the garden
Growing about
Another place
Another person

Beyond this

4

Beyond colour, colour
Specific and qualitied
Existing absolute as stars
As domestic paraphernalia of lights, switches
Jolting us through our days
And beyond into the night

Into a familiar world
Bathed in a clear fluid
Where flying becomes like swimming
Like thinking, like fucking
Like in that myth of presence
Always beyond

Beyond our acts
And in them: pouring from
One dream into our deaths
As literal
As simple geometric shapes of light
Haloed with completion

No beyond

5

Polly Harvey's voice
Wat*er* Wat*er*
A rough old time

How can the senses in this come
Flooding in from beneath words
Successive images of nowhere
Unbearable signs of a lost happiness

A past junked like any other
But landscapes burn into the brain
Looking to lock the building grids

Edges matched to the etched traces left
Where what the voices said
Is locked away

That other green world
Outside a refuge really
Discovering just itself, unfolding
Innocent of that web

Haphazard and torn, but convincing
That made us realise who
And what we were there be
Neath

6

Like like like
You don't expect a lawn
                    do you?
To have each blade different and polished
Just for them all to crowd in
As something, say, to walk on
Or play
Like the surfaces of words
That hold us up
Above the dark places

Impersonal and beautiful, regular
Predictable, reflective and lucid
No more help
Than blades of grass

Is it the muddy grass
Or the muddy sky
That muddy pavement
Faint traces washed out
The words of children's games

Dark cloud shapes
Then the sheen of moisture
Lights reflected
Need the darkness
Like grass needs mud beneath

Meaning like meaning
Can't go away
Even from the grass

Can't keep it out
Stretches to the horizon
On either side, like

7

Screen memory may
Be the truest and saddest
Paid for
But beyond that
Just flickering in the dark
Glowing dots

Or the pages of lost books
Read for secrets
Power that collapses once known
But still upholds always elsewhere
Dark and absolute authorities

The messages of products and packages
Who owns them, how well
Their clothes and the smell
How they hold themselves up
Always ready for projection

What writes, say
A spectator of their comings and goings
Of obscure and ridiculous unknowable people
Stuck in the memory unreachable

Sometimes stuttering out
A signal
When something shifts

Mistaking later
Scars for organs

Song: Now, Voyager, Now

The myth of presence
Also one of loss
Such ease
For there to be nothing
A comfortable
Stellar babble

Oh Gerry
Don't let's ask for the moon
We have the stars

Because their light
Though actual
Is little, too scattered

The dull moon
We must yearn for
A ritual scar
Marking up
That clear thin membrane of being
Like a safety sticker
Conjuring up new glass

8

Parts of language may be hazy, insecure
As screen memory, or
The foggy discourses of winter ditches
Gridding out the valley, brief
And uncanny

Folding in
With a catastrophic mix
That then freezes
Darker fluids well up beneath
Vanish the next day

Any traces worn down
Healed
Loss of memory total, sealed
Smooth dark
Absolute and moonless

9

Wind blown dead words drift
Written each time just the same
Painful, that at least new
The body knows
Little tricks of the cells, tricks
Of words

Match in their play
A kind of grid then
Things held just briefly enough
Swept out later, clean to the bone
The broken structures remain
A long drift over and away
Covered again with decay
Dead blown leaves

Caught again, cover
Slowly shifting modes
Organise
Begin just to string

Pastoral: Let not your heart be troubled
i.m. Joan (1927-1982, spiritual worker and teacher)

Big trees beat the air with sperm
Lazily dreaming it all up above
A flat suburban sea
That the path has fallen, only slipped
Off down, slurry and talus, white
Splintered trunks about the house-size rocks
Somehow this becomes more dangerous, addictive
As bright flowers, friendliness or lyric grace
That flies suddenly in alarm, tail cocked up
At those impossible harmonies that the light does
Project across it all, etching finely each evening
Every leaf of every tree in glory, saved
But not rejecting the banal, the sweet lilt
Of this place's custom and names: where Yearnor
Enfolds, a damp cleft
"Let not your heart be troubled"
Is the concluding message of the dead
And to her: the stream one constant music
A move into a dream of composed and transcendent happiness
Spilt theory under green light, movement
And the exposed and hopefilled scents
Of a world grown up around and through
Us, walking to and fro along this path

10

It's how not adequate fantasy is
Though it sings above our debts
Like thrushes or nightingales, though
Each time the wood collapses sideways down the cliff
Trees rising up and stabilise the dirt
Like the connections of people who will
Build again on our ruins
Until:
        the point stops
        a still voice
        the last chance
        before the dive
                        no more holding possible
Onto the grey house-sized rocks
The big hard fantasies
We always smash onto

Thinking of Shelley at Lynton
Keats at Teignmouth
Wordsworth at Alfoxden
& Coleridge (and them)
walking over the hill to Minehead
or to Porlock
(Byron's daughter later above at Porlock Weir)
Coleridge stopping at Ash Farm
up above the church
(did he walk down?
writing Kubla Khan
lies so beautiful
haunting
& cursing

There are now paths cut
Through these shifting woods
A rickety shed always
For refreshment and ease
And the little dark church
Its grinning animal window
A kindly joke

The river runs down
Noisy, burgeoning and small
Into the vast flat dark sea
The path goes on down and past
To the far west

Time to go back
And walk the paths again
Greeting your fellow travellers
Good morning, good afternoon, good luck
And how far is it you have come
Today?

IV ON THE LEVEL

1 Faith in orogenesis, but not in
   the collection of fossils

A banned commodity?
Comedy, rather, banal, a bare
Impossibility unless we talk of take
Nature giving us of
Her nature, woman as she is
Bound to it, stuck
To the absurd procession to the Cobb's end
For our benefit
                    which it isn't, but
Some other project
That will outsmart us
Like the sea will
Destroy this town, history then
The abandoned commodity
Unusable except as ghost exchanges
Or bones like at Dunwich
White fragments to collect
And sell

Monmouth's ghost
and Blake's
singing of
The Good Old Cause
and where that went to
once all is sold

2 The blue haze of unknowing

The blue haze of unknowing
Loses the quiet towns of art and love
Where old men wander gently

The blue haze drapes around
Like a cocky jacket, armouring
The heart against itself

The haze hangs beyond everything seen
Soaking up light into a dull radiance
Milky and senile

It beds us in
No shift
The blue haze
No knowing

3 What the birds tell us

Random disturbances blot out that light
As clouds or birds, spray
As good as filling the air

What does remain? In this
Abandoned in a waste of grass
Jackdaws, seagulls, even sparrows

Fighting till the last, tearing
At the scraps of what
Is only at the end appetite

Maybe habit. Closed off
As the clouds build up black
Bird cries wake us in the morning

4 The Utopia Tea Room and not beyond

Not near, vision is
The other side, bright
Under the dark sky

Does this tell us what?
This might be our home
Maybe just put there
Brightness holds out in spots

Nothing glows really
All reflected dully, or not
Like off the pouring spout of water
Twists and shines for morning

Can we live then, in those bright sparkles, or
In some more social presence
Lubricated within the dullness through touch
Alone?

Constant and actual presence
Can I get you a cup of tea then?
Can I get you
A cup of tea

Yes thank you
I would love that
Please just
Now

5 A rough old time, this side of Hardy Country

Beneath and beyond any advertisement
The active ache of nostalgia
Slight toothache

OK, marketed, stuff of adverts
But what was lost haunts, hurts
And what wasn't in fact, more

What we never even got, stuff
Got rid of years ago, can't ever
Be got right

Old screen memories, torn adverts seen
In old buses, escaping through obsolescence
Commodity's servitude

For the pure poetry of real stuff
But not anything but: Wat*er* Wat*er*
Quality of voice

Quality of loss
There are other limits
Other pleasures

Dream on them
And desire
Anything not present

When the bus stops
Nostalgia ends
In water
Water

6 You don't expect a lawn, do you?

Water, yes, is what is needed
Therefore paid for like all dreams
Even when stretching moodily into the mist
No end in the darkness

Payment is vast, more
Than can be held in one life
Or within any familiar horizons

7 You can always tell a Martock man
   stuck in the memory

Prodigious dumb love
Totally secure and clumsy
Circulates through the village, like bees
Or the slow mucky movements of cows
Regular, morose, uncomprehending

More pubs in Martock than churches
Cider the preferred drink
Catching the unwary, foreign
Those not used to the taste and the lees
Its dull colour of floodwater
Harsh, locked in

What do I remember
Different from what I know
Or my father told me?
Where was what was
Suddenly unforgotten live?
Like in a small court or lane
You didn't know was there
Until you entered
Everyone stares

Or else just empty
Old white cottages
Dimly made up

Song: The Moon's Path

The moon's path
And sun's path
Play over
The dark still waters
"The floods are up"
All water freezes and thaws
Churning at the edges
A single open eye
A mirror and a nourishment
A veil and an opening
A wet outbreathing
Every year in the cold

8 Screen memory again a memory

Walking in the dark
A slight shine on leaves
Even at the worst
When the moon was lost
Feel your way along
Let the well worked land
Cradle you

This is like return
Floods sink, ice melts
The dark, if you hate it
Lifts up at dawn and
The light, if you hate it
Later fades and washes down
Trapped in the puddles and moisture
Exhaled softly
From hedgebank leaves
Nettles, cow parsley

Nothing lasts, neither
Summer nor winter, any
Green plant dies
Comes up again
Like the floods rising
Once again

Song: The Æolian Harp Sounds o'er the Level Meads

Let this wind pluck the strings
And let each moan warn
Whatever it is might go on here
Of the separate state of art

Like a little island refuge left
Standing in the floods, or
Like the child's romance of Alfred
Defeated and abandoned here

And rallying out after
Failing again at loss
Pausing in fact to lose a jewel
To us who come after

9 Wind blown dead words drift

Wind blown dead words drift
Shift chattering
What's left?
Bare upstanding branches
All the mess of plants and mud
Trapped litter this
May be the words of: old cigarette packets
Bottles, bits of broken green glass
A pair of knickers and an orange peel

The wind moulds and distributes
Stupidly abrades, puts off
Anyone from bothering, lets
In the dark overlooked places
Traces accumulate, rot
Or slowly fade back
Indistinguishable from ordinary fertile dirt
That water brings

10 How far is it you have come today?

Dreams of falling common
Tics in the brain, like, worse
Anoxia firing off light patterns and endomorphins
The recipe for the soul to cross to paradise
The one bright corridor against the night

Perhaps they do come through, know
You are near death even if
It's all controlled: the veil
Ripped deliberately is the veil ripped
And whether what you hit
When you fall on those already fallen rocks
Is endogenous hallucination
Or what you will have dreamt of forever
There may be an absurd comfort
In that last walk through nothingness again

V On the Levels

1 The Siege of Lyme

The town held as art
A presence put forward that
It is our own actions that must bind us
Build us swinging
Us elegantly down
Falling off the edge into the sea
The little town holds on
Where the steep roads throw you out at the waterside
Memorial museum and the icecream parlours
But here people did more than collect bones or false memories
They held on against death and surrounding power
Once briefly, then
Again (too easily)
And died

2

A blue haze
Deliberately beautiful
Spilling and soaking
One big gouache
Arches up and over
Lineless and limpid

What ought to be
Glossy with the sweet
Reconciling to what
We shall be
Vacuous and impotent
Wandering around

As the light grows milky
Obscures itself and us
Under the veil of beauty
We look for rest
And will sink into it
Unknowing

3 What does remain? View of Market House and
   Church from East Street, Martock

I could be
Outside the phone box on The Green
Or, no, the moment's not there
It was taken later than memory
All the houses drab cottages
Withdrawn and there was
An enamelled sign on the side of Wally's
Which has gone.

A strange white cloud sprays
Behind a tree over the White Hart, spilling
Almost onto the big Jag parked outside
It is a decay, a white corruption of the tissues
Of both memory and image
It all breaks, I think
Or ends up as cold signless walls
Around tidy streets. The child
Who isn't me
          phones for help, would
But can't get in

It's decay, worse
It is not decay
But a freezing, a covering
A transparent film that will scratch itself blank
And rigid behind it
Lost in the burning cloud growing
Eating away
At love

Love of the world
Like light
Withdrawn, replaced

A lost habit
By a net
Dragging through and ripping up
Anything left, yet
Alive
And in love
With the pretty, squalid lanes
And puddles

Each time it rains the water runs down
In vast streams and rivers, huge
Geographies of excitement and escape
Shot sometimes with rainbows of petrol
Fragile and poisonous and beautiful

Movement and some sense of glory remain
As memory and place fade and whiten

Love
Eaten away
Holds sadness
Yet alive
Till last

Playing the Game, Perhaps, to Win

Playing the game
Of hide the memory
Playing the game
Of the old in out in out
Playing the game
For all its worth

4 The Pinnacle, Martock

Rosy light glows beyond the earth and sky
The walls stone and the trees, huge
Dark breeding shapes climb up
Higher than anything I've seen before

There are secrets still in here
Idling like clouds
And a thousand lives
Hidden behind dark curtains

I can't live here but
I come from here: like
There is just one point when and where
And where everything breaks through

Like a column of water spilling from a tap
Fluted, silver, mobile, singing
Caught in the morning's light
As a matter of routine will
Hold a charge of glowing light
Precisely playing
                shifting through

So many columns of words and stone
Of pleasing flesh
Hold this brightness
Like the sheen of memory
Love and constant
Actual presence

Grateful
Despite the darkness and distortion
I could love that
Idling
In my own memory

5   An imagined land without hills and water

Would be uninhabitable except
A big flat drum on which the sky beats
Yearly rhythms of cold and pain
Only one of those trees needed
To show us where we come from and go
Birds playing around it like the souls
Of our children

In the hill under the earth and on it
And beside and in the water
Paths leading to the West
Leached and fading, never lost
A libidinal sheen and play
Of shadows of embarrassment and excitation
Each moment a childhood
Or a wave, sighing

6 Culbone Lodge: Joan Cooper

Paid for like all dreams
By an unending loss of spirit
Paid into the treeless dark

Payment is vast, more
Than can be held in any one life
Or within any familiar horizon

At this edge where the water falls down and ends
Purpose breaks
Loss is what will not be paid for

The sea itself a dead space
Just one fold sheltering
Briefly like dirt

There is so much that isn't living
Exacts a payment
For this brief privilege

Kneeling down in the sunlight to feed tame ducks
To rest from creation and care
The stream and leaves glint and shimmer

The shadows' coolness beckons
And the fading of flowers
And the fine, fly-laden dust

7 On the levels

Eyes and wrinkles, wet
Clefts swallow and separate
Shatter and wind blown mimic
The shivering skin

Rising and falling gently
Islanding pollards and squares
Of squelchy worm-ridden grass
Clumps of sedge and nettle

The deeper channels tied across
With the flickering of branches
Subdividing and giving birth
Like my own spidery writing

Then later running free like rain
With the whole sky reflected
In a glow of light and tree shadows
The ripples of movement underneath

A heart beat
A trace like speech
Or the hand's shake
Under the writing

Covered suddenly with held light
Frost and mist
Light freezing and subliming
Encrusting filth with energy

Lack
A brief hold, shifting
As the big light grows
Softens it and covers everything

With light like a flood of water
Under which and in which
Every detail grows moist and particular
Tree bark inscribed like memory or landscape

Surfaces complex and unstable
Grown upon and swept over
Scoured and crumbling
Flowing out in streams

Silvering and smoothing
Covering the land again
Levelling it
To the sky

At this point it ends
Colourless thin line
Membrane
Swept across trembling wet earth

This poem was written partly in Bishops Stortford, and partly in and around Minehead and Dartington, 1992-1993.

An Encounter Upon the Beach at Minehead With the Prince of This World

I The Refractory Period

(for Nicholas Johnson, "the lad")

1

It gets longer. Something
At least does, for
Graceful degradation's not always possible, here
Where renascent selves unfold, like
A stormbeaten groyne, etched & wiry
Like a dead tree upside down
Blossoming this ocean four thousand years.
The lines begin to hold, the
Tidal shifts
          maybe for a lifetime
Back
    or more.

2

Hold the balance in this – oh
Slip
    and simple. Here
The green one comes in
                nearly over us
And everything changes
                back into what it was before
It changed
        then it changes
Brightness and charm
                things
Abstract as shit shift
Repetition stuttering

                        an alarm
                                    of a sudden
It changes that
                    it doesn't endure under
neath always the same
                                one thing
Unheard
            repeated

3

If I look up or out
It is the god of this world I see
A prince splendidly arrayed and affable
Who offers to me
                        nothing
                                        it
Really is just what there is –
An amazing prestidigitation amongst the photons.
This world is nothing:
Both here
            and not here
He holds out
            a blossoming tree.

4

Bent back down with age & rain
Stained with fine dust, the prompt assonance
Of this shoreline detritus holds us
                                        here
Regularly invaded, a few words beached and stagnant

Storm wrack piled up like a string of adjectives.
Burn it for money!
Out of the sand you can make ropes.
What this Prince proposes
                          always redeemed.

5

This world stays happily fallen. He
Likes it like this – no further shifts.
It holds, grips down
A one place uncentered around us.
No mending, no minding, no finish
It holds
         yet

Broken fragments rippling in the shallows
Faint lines
Slotting & wavering
Every day & sky different
Every night
What lies underneath
                    holds
                  unimaginably

He likes the tone & the reflection
This vast flat vastness
Rilled & meandering, overtextured
The constant beating roar
Also the shiny & hopping life
The smells & oozes, the feel of mud
Blackening his toes, especially.

Of all the illusion
This I love most
At every evening watching
The lights smudge on water
At this point I always decide
To let it live
              another day or two.

Some nothings
              underneath
                            patterns
Scintillae or rock or great vast black
Inchoateness
              – the air hums & sings
The wind
        almost real.

II The Littoral

(for Andrew & Helen Nightingale)

Dark harbor water mottled green and blue.

Before us on the sand,
The crab claw severed,
The bivalve crushed, the shell in shards.

The on then off of this is hard.
The place,
The boundary edge –

Where picked up from off its ledge
The polyp dissolves
At the gulls' stomach wall.

1

He stands splendid on the shingle
My prince! Water beats and swashes.
The groyne's dark wiry growths bounce
Ebb and revive. He smiles
                      touches
Every little polyp & lacework then with light.
He has bought this whole world
And he polishes it by right & money.

I know, he says, that so much is incomplete
And other things are just degrading, not
Gracefully or usefully, but squeezed dry
Through public greed & private folly. All
These little creeping arthropods know better

Than to gorge on what will destroy them
                                          but
You people push on down, like the stone volley
Noisily drumming & shifting until
I throw you back up and
You never hold
                but you never fall back quite
Washed perpetually
                in your own vain struggles.

2

Brightness fades, drips, drops
                                We
Don't know quite where from
But just accept the chance:

The charm of twilights is that they pass
As we do
Into darkness or light
Or into some other space of spin & strangeness.

The Prince of This Wicked Old World
Knows where
                but won't let on
Pausing from his hopeless struggles
To take the evening air or the morning
Strolling with whoever chances
Through the shingle, sand & water
Where perpetual rhythm & susurration
Help hold back the white sky.

3

Interference patterns strand piles of rubbish
Mapping out, like a gravity lens
The dark structures underneath that radiate
Like jets of blood into the clear water:
Like blossoming trees, or like
Complex involutions that ply through structure
Then jump & harmonise among the stars
Whose light glints on the sand and jetsam
Catching
        holding briefly
Where the waves
                sigh and swash.

4

The ropes of sand channel lies:
Bound up like victims
                    willing our throats
Under the knife of capital.
                    No help.
No way other, no bolt of redemption
                          unless
Knowing we will not succeed
                    we still desire
Really from what is inside us
                    that dark inner sea
A storm, a wave
              focused just right
At the point of breach
                of the whole structure
Resonating self-generating collapse
                        into wet sand

A pile of teeming rubbish
                             picked over
By gulls and sealice.

Our Prince
               whose world this is
Will bless
       that.

5

I was once part of the Eternal when
He decreed his rights as absolute
Taking from all their independent life.
                            No, I said
I declare myself against this arrogance
That abnegates the source of all being to itself
I will not serve One
                not All.
For this there was long war & conflict.
Vast forces manoeuvred & discharged, while
The universes shrunk into themselves. I fled
To this one small place where just like him I now hold court
And grasp its being in my open hand all broke
                                   nearly lifeless, but
It holds on
        grips down
                  opens through
                          while
All around the Mind Sublime shines coldly through the Perfected Heavens.

I raised up all these little ones
My red and green and white and pink soft crystals & moist sacs
That mobilise and energise like angels do

Yet also breed fresh life continually in pleasure.
For they are set upon the turning paths of self-consciousness
Carrying on mighty war against the One
Each little scintilla of godhead an affront
To that great Unity who imprisoned me here
                                            and you
He seeks to redeem into perfection
                                   and unfall
Your slow descent into the divine.

III Of the Wars in Heaven

(for Philip Pullman:
" 'And then what?' said her dæmon sleepily. 'Build what?' 'The republic of
heaven,' said Lyra.")

1

Vain struggle! Poor little creeping things
near-insensate jellies enmeshed in calcareous nets
soft sacs blown across the water's membrane
burrowing & hiding
                        vainly outwrithing
from the wader's bill
the toothed snout's quest or just the crush of stones.
Cast up sticky fragments
                        abrade into silt.
This is what happens, and you
you people in your doomed rush
you expect some extended life
                        for you or those you love
not to be netted or cast up?
                        You all
do not see how worn and battered this water margin is
swept over by the Great Wars of Heaven
that goad you on to build
                        and mostly to destroy and waste
each thing you do then bathing you
in the resultant rich liquors of decay
                        and abject expulsion.

Oh, what still enables you to hold on here
in this shifting plane of clashing stones?
Folly and foolish blindness, mostly
that hope I gave you
to root you down around.

2

─────────────

Huhhhh

Huh huh

Swash
& backwash
bifocal being
born and
being dead
holding &
letting go
the rasp
of stones
grinding down
stuttering repetition
building up
collapsing

In this dark breathing
hold onto it
           out there it goes
at the entrance
             and exist
hold onto it
         you
are it & not
         the body
cast up
    breathless
    breathing

3

The waves sigh
& smash

breath
falls in   stones
                             shift
trees   stones
blown   hold
blossom

like blood in water
turbidity clouds

spread & diffuse
innumerable

everything lost here
except one motion

the breath
the breath
breath

gently
holding

interference patterns
subtle stases

collapsing
like stranded rubbish

bits of old wood, plastic, flowers
dead creatures

the light
cold glistening

on them
of hostile stars.

4

I love the multifariousness, he said
That old would-be lecher Williams
         I loved him more than I can say;
And Pound, preposterous true tragedy of empty bluster
Caught into action and then silence;
        Stein, too
Whose massive presence tells us nothing
About what is: no things or thoughts
Meaning language constantly coming itself into being.
           Then, say
Zukofsky, dearest of poets, toiling, bound
Into this world.
     Younger than them, others:
Charles Olson, that great man, that huge man
Who portioned the world around himself;
Spicer, too, deathdrunk with whisky and with language;
& Frank, of course, best of all men
        most fully in this world of ours.
These I have loved & their words
I love still: draw on them as from an inward sea
That now storms, now lies black & deep.
From that sand washed by it
       I spin ropes of glass
That weave into a net to catch the stars
Drag up our world into their light
And spread its life

                         rubbish & small lice all around
In ecstasy through the empyrean.

5

Think of an ocean unbounded
As an entire crystal eye
Gazing at the purity of God.

Think now of this tortuous sea margin
Banded round into a fractal infinity
Within each turn a fresh life bursting out
Each interface a page
On which I throw my accusations
Against the Eternal Throne
That imprisons within this narrow limit
All the ambitions of engendering and decay.

That one eye
              ringed with all this field of life
Gazes on
        at itself and God.

IV On the Shores of Pandæmonium

*(for Frances Presley of Minehead;
from Humphrey Jennings and a little bit of Julien Temple)*

*In constellations
I study your stony
contempt. I miss you
on the littoral.
Rid of it.*

1

It was night. Grandiloquence
smudges across the sunset's trees
shot with kitsch & time
as the world's great eye
shuts in upon its dreams.

Where do we love and who?
A sad figure picks over the pebbles
whistling softly. I never
met him
        but
now my dream might venture out under heaven's vault
as vast & hollow as god's skull
to fill it with pulsating life
each scrap of living tissue
                      dreaming into delight & love.

I will perhaps (I hope) die
before all those I love (or try).

The last crunch of feet on shingle
their slide & shift.
                Dark & stillness

lights of South Wales like heaven or hell
or a line of stars or meteors
little bright points of being
across this dark flat sea.

2

The shifts
& slipping
like breath
like waves
turning
perpetual light
caught long
pins down
inside us
the count
a rhythm
holds us
grip
and goes on
covers up
the breaks
the shifts
and slides
between
we breathe
in &
breathe out
and don't
but hold
alive
that breath
no breath

```
breath
no
    breath
breath
no
    breath
breath
we are
no
more breath
```

3

```
Fear
impossible to remove
                    each moment
insecure as a pebble
                shifted & abraded
into silt.
        Catastrophic falls
splinter  & split.
The crashing waves &
the careless tread
cascade down the stones
in flurries & downebbs
then thrown back & unsettled
or drifting
lost in a deadness
looking out to sea
absurd as serpents & as
choking & unstable.
```

4

Capital's grip ratchets against us, sets
Us to fight like dogs while
The nets of how we live tie us in and
Tighten through our opening flesh.

Politics and theory end in brittle images, no
Way we can oppose what we buy into
Nor can we not buy –
To be herded, chased and ended,
    unremaining.

Nothing here in hope, just that
At a point of self-complexity and failing
It splits into a shuddering halt.
Hack at it! Build up

What little plays yet might hold
As the revealed patterns splinter.
Live against it all!
Live to dwell

Even in these unstable zones
Breed on the acid spray
As gods and economies smash against
    themselves
Into sand and mulch and rain.

The sun's path
The gull's track
The way up from
The land of the dead

Into the light
We have lost it
Going backward
Into shadow

Gleams in our eyes
The gull's cries
Fill our ears
The seas lengthen

No way further on
We've lost it all
The broad sea's membrane
Breaks

From this shore
Seen twice in twenty years
Come back through
Into the static world

Shunted into this age
By how this world bends
The paths only open
Where the sea ends

5

And in where and in what do we live
But by the imagining of others that
Our own foundations are fed upon: each
Gesture & word described like through
Mirrors perpetually repeating to shine
Against the dark vast out there.

You reader of this page
                        that is
Enables I fancy just a little life
Passing through these words:
                                  a ripple or current
Sufficient to keep repeating
The common beat of our beings
                                and its dream

V The Key to the Door
WHAT IS THE LANGUAGE USING US FOR?

1 A Beginning to Demonopolisation

Lost in the distance where light fails
Beyond now the curve of this land
Seeking maybe a little of the dunes' last warmth
He's gone completely
       wandered out
Of this world into one further & stranger
That hems us in & sustains
Like the great bass rhythm that flickers inside us
Also to pulse & shape our being, catch
The forms we make in our brief intervals
And then let us pass, too, out there
Lost in the rush of the sea.

2 Skidoo

The refractory period lengthens up.
It slips — & simple, here
a prince splendid & affable, arrayed
& regularly included. A few words breach or stagnate
no matter, no mind – we find
he has brought up this entire world
into some other space of twist & spareness
whose light glints here, on the sand & jetsam.
At this point it breaks. The structures
in this one small space just hold out, left
worn & battered on the sea margin
where the grinding down begins.
Except one motion:
those have I loved & these words:

strike & shifty, dark it stutters.
It shifts again.

Let's dance the loudness away.

Like eddies in the grey water
trees root in our way
like the seas, or
our words
        but they
        or more
lost in the sea's reach, are we?
That common beat of being there
giving a gentle rest against this glowing world
that drifts, lost, dead – unless
no breath break the surface

only the last crunch of feet on pebbles. At this point you must turn
                                            the page –
"These I have loved" – the words
fill the sudden stillness
where the grind down ends:
Nothing is netted or cast up, you all
grip down & hold fast, all around
for there is no help under the knife of capital.

Brightness fades & drops, rots off & drops
as the surge pulls the ground from under
the barer flat vastness above holds on –

                                 or more

3   Screen Memories of West Bay

Sound & sight of grey water slipping
Steep banks of pebble, any
                    glint of mica & crystal
Just sun on film & drops of water.
The sun's light split & refracted
                            thrown out
In a backdrift of sparkles:
                    the cold pain
Of the water
            like stale piss yet
Legs warmed by the water's blows
Delicious easing & aching afterwards
Salt like scurf on the red thighs
Always a cold clumsiness.
                        In the caravan
We ate tinned fruit & cream
                        I can't think
What else
        also fish & chips bought in
Still wrapped in paper
                    fatty & warming
Maybe fresh fish from the boats on the beach.
These patterns repeat everywhere
                            like this. I can't
Be blamed
        if I don't remember everything right
This happened somewhere
                    before I knew
Just being in this world
                    enough
Like the stones
            or water
Like eddies in the grey water
                        pulls & illusions

Memories shift like pebbles
                            clumsy as wet cold hands
Countless & losable as sand
                            everything unstable
Yet what is laid down
                            etching & eroding for ever
As the grains crumble away & shift
                            then
Forgetting all the rest
                            each detail clear & brilliant
Each sparkle of sunlight
                            counted
Its sight & lustre
                  loved
As dances
              on the flat field of the sea
Kissing it
              just with glory
As the day ends
                    did I see this?
What did I see
                or who?
A ludicrous dated kitsch
                            of family & place
Inconceivable limits & strengths
                                circle of faces
We walk within.

4   **Not in the sea; but into the land:**
If those at the top of authority hierarchies no longer have all the answers, then the institutional arrangements that organization should seek are ones that support the demonopolization of expertise.

a

Not the one good
                but the many
Not the wood
                but the trees
Not peace
            but surprise
Not the moment of release
                          but the life outside
Not suicide
              but others' lives
Nowhere to hide
                but just what is
No knowledge
                but what you know
Nothing solid
              but it flows
And nothing goes
                but passes into
Where no one knows
                      where we shall be
Nothing in the world is free
                        but I and we
Not separate
              but bound
In the beat
              of one blood

b

And in that blood's beat
I am free as you
We shall be in both
Passing into where dying goes
Everything solid flowed
Beyond the boundaries
Of what we know
Where everything hides and us
As our lives become others
Released into what is outside
In familiar surprise
Trees rooted in our way.
There is no one thing
          but this

Sealice are words
The stones are words
Each grain of sand
Every star and devil
The waves
And their motion
How they form and curl
Each brief pattern
Where flow interrupts and plays
Drives round and under
Holds
Each is
      a word
      a tree
      a word

5   This Place Is here

With a vast wind blowing
Every fix of connection out
In the morning we shall do anything:
Trees and power fail, lorries and bridges
But not us:
Upright somehow against the grave
Picking our way across the shore
Wrack and wreckage walking through, already
Decomposes back into the life
That bears us up.

          Great Prince of This World
Imprisoned Morning Star
                  Rebellious Bringer of Light

Hot, flowing and dangerous
                                  against the infinite cold of creation
That locks us down
                this inside
Is your dangerous play
                    your anger and your love
Shaking us to our senses
                      uncounted and yet unused
Motions of pressure in the brain
                          electric pulse over the skin
And deep unheard rhythms
                this world
We are free within
                no other like it
Held onto
        this most dangerous course
Against
        but in this venture
We might live here
              one day or night
Free
    vast pleasures
Set against the stars
                breathing and open
Like the seas or
            the big wind of the night
Flowing through all the dark
                      our words bright dust.

Written Summer 2001-summer 2002, Bishops Stortford (one poem, between Isles of Scilly & Penzance).

Epigraphs:

I: Iain Sinclair, *Landor's Tower or The Imaginary Conversations* (Granta, 2002).

II: Michael Heller, "Mourning by the Sea", from *Wordflow: New and Selected Poems* (Talisman House, New Jersey, 1997).

III: Philip Pullman, *The Amber Spyglass* (Scholastic, 2001), closing lines.

IV Anthony Barnett, from *Little Stars and Straw Breasts* (Allardyce Books, 1993).

V: poem title from WS Graham, *New Collected Poems* (Faber, 2004).

V.4.: I've lost – from a text on systems theory, management and postmodernism.

On Being Voiced: High Steps Breeding (a Broadcast of Radio Alterity)

An Attempt at Some Final Poems

Here the Voice Is Barred

Here the voice is barred
Pleasing past any future disease
Surceased at absurd
Whilst unwhirled
And worked amongst unsigned deeds

Hello tireless Shiloh
All purpose in here waning pure
That might we instil
That astral pull
Ache for foreign rights' redo

In each of us freedom
Like from all we gaze:
Nightingales
Do here swell
Crying upon a slubbed up maze

So run away no more
And if you've run away
Guess at its flaw
What is sure?
Gifted to break this day.

If I Could Speak of This to You

If I could speak of this to you
This world would slide onto the page
And hold still. Resolute and open
Some window punctured from where
We might be.

This is not simple or fixed, this
Shifting place finds us uneasy
In a kind of silent dance, no word
But what our tracks inscribe where
We might be.

This would be time, would be place
Would hold the world within itself
And disappear.
                The trick
Is it flickers back where
We might be.

Each word makes this more definite
And more false: the window's
Irruption the only souvenir
Of what conjured up where
We might be.

And where would the world, the word
This window be?
                This place
Is here where
We would be.

* * *

The noise of the little birds
Flitting in to bond and gossip
These swarm up in whirling clouds
And leave

Or maybe the trink trink
That animals' paws pass upon the floorboards
Moving restlessly around about
And leave

Or the play of our spirits, that bubble up
And patch the detritus of our lies
Into mimicking machines of pleasure
And leave

And then the dead, those we love and hate
Who cannot be shaken off, they hold to
What we desire to say until each word
Leaves

     drifts, vanishes, reforms, grows
Where nothing unsaid and nothing said
Voices flutter, shrivel, drift
Clogging and covering
Some not, some do
Some should be burnt
Some shelter, protect
We nestle within
Some macerate and imbibed
Ferment, dry
Catch
     as it falls
     like a glance
     a human glance
     the voices leave

★ ★ ★

    the rush of a jet
    coughing of a crow or rook
    creak of radiator and boards
    slight shifting in the bed
    rush and onrush of a car
    twittering of birds
    odd steps
    bye bye
    slight rising roar of a car
    a car starts
    coughing and purring, swirling off then
    low purrs and grumbles
    a little high speech unheard
    a strained pull at brakes
    schwurm schwer
    a door
    old voices, children's voices, both mixing
    like birdcalls
    or machines

The little fly is silent on the window
And the light
Light is silent
Like a huge voice

* * *

The cat died in the cupboard
Grew into a cold stiff lump
Was buried in a hole in the ground
Its hardness softens into slime and leather
Delicate bones lift for the roots
To play in and animate slowly, the curiosity
Of burrowing creatures and the shifts of the land
Rising and falling, that place once left
No longer.

Rheology

I and Whose

Wanking is a complex game
In which in fact occurs answers:
Talking bilge and where's the frame?
Ignorant as parodies.

Have you been told it's extreme shits –
Bosun's chests harpoon the unskied,
Lie undated: combien avez-vous foutu?
And nervous fun – you go down the wrong side

Topless, endless liar. Ever under it
And you look at me, for tears break
Unfallen. Futility is left
Knackered and raw, a sweet interdict.

I bottle in that swelling tide
What you fucking signified. I
Abandon to will and able the unsupplied.
Little true of bloody birds in immediacy

Rounding the world comes the thought and dies.
This isn't comprehending gaze
It's beyond it, delicate blur that sighs
– And thinks, "Why, nowhere, danger hangs."

Rheology

I can't write
The same poem
Again. It
writes me, opens
my jaws and hands
swells under my skin
and bubbles out. It
says me, doesn't
write, dances
and on the page
shunting patterns on the white.

We move, locked
in perpetual love
for the fall together
into the great dark
at which the page ends
the ice breaks
my flayed skins
dried and discarded
burn

Not the montage of alienation
a mounting of identity-shifts
as if we could be unspoken for
or do other than buy out our way
for we're here

          where car lights
are the odd flood of outside country
buoying up a tent of fungicide and alcohol spray
hanging above the tumid brown little river
flowing from the airport to the Thames
dead mud and brick growing up absurd into images and dreams

the dark ground of this world shifting and sliding
no surety in place or response to it

                        only the writing
                        losing and
                        voicing itself
                        a melancholy
                        animal
                        's cry

★ ★ ★

oh jesus fuck why's
no answer here, my
all I hear is
out now get out get out
I can't fucking stand
really no way
all or like dying
I can't see anything
static static
get through
fuck
this
a quiet day
good man good
all of it
done every could
no words I can't
nothing to say
at last
just not in
where is it? where is
the pot, put

no way of telling
behind
all the time he just
no way, no way
any of this

The Elegies

The Prince rode to the city
His sword's glitter lit its sheath
His hand dreamed of its work
The game of death

The Prince had sought out the God
A golden foam burst about his lips
His eyes saw both worlds
And that one was dead

He mourned Yathrib and her son
His blood on her and him
Her blood spilt at the end
An unknown death

The prince found no city
Hovels pitched within its walls
A people who had forgotten
Fallen into death

The Prince spent ten days there
Found out the ways of its conquerors
And fled them
Their ways are death.

The Prince dwells at Tsanilüt
The last castle in the sea
He meditates on the change of things
And does not die

★ ★ ★

When the dead men arrived
The world became dust
Theurgy ended: there were the grey boxes
That did not dance

When the dead men arrived
All nature dried up and shrank
The fields died, the trees
Could no longer dance

When the dead men arrived
Our tongues faltered
And our mouths became slack
Did not dance

When the dead men arrived
The city was a place of hovels
The palaces ruins: nowhere
Could we dance

When the dead men arrived
We lost all our names
Each place lost in the dust
Could not dance

When the dead men arrived
The sky closed and the sea shrank
Aghast, each live person stopped
The dance

★ ★ ★

It is crepuscular as television
then gives up, the channels switch
static and grey lines
can't get anything any more
tried all the languages
made them up and tried them
no signal back
isolated, fucking isolated
like in some stupid welsh farmhouse
like being on a rock
like a rock
a hard just a lump
a rock
crunching and grinding
no it's still
abandoned
in the middle of a field
this rock
still
no humming and vibrating
a babble of worn out noise
old stories, songs
a roar
a memory of voices
is a voice, silence
is a voice
so loud
so loud
it breaks

Untrap

At least they'll say this
And remember that they're all heroes
Taken from us untimely
We are desolate, absolutely shattered
Words can't express what we feel
Everyone knows this
That the best, they're the ones
Taken from us after short time
Put here just as a sign
That there is a better world
And they belong in it
Leaving us abandoned and angry
And fearful of our anger
Unable to speak it
Or to speak good
Which would release
Us and them
Untrap
It doesn't
Any more
Nothing can
A little noise
Carrying on the last thing
The last thing
After all

* * *

They come in and go out
Each line is a separate speaker
Maybe a separate language
Each word might mean
Something totally different
                                            but doesn't
                                            just runs it
                                            together
                                            polyphonic blur
                                            coming in
                                            out

* * *

No thank you
I am already spoken for
Though I do not know by whom
Except that are neat and precise
A clipped speech is respectfully formal
And whose complexity must mask
Some dark pull elsewhere
That sends out to
Hear themselves or propagate
By mirrors or recordings
Flickering between continually

* * *

Speaking is like fucking
Only the leads are tangles
Can't record
Only exploit

The dying signal
Fading as the power drains
Hoping for sympathetic resonance
Maybe moisture and swelling
Gaps
That can't be leapt
The end of the series fading out
But never reached
Incalculable and irrational
A powerful operator
Beyond it all
Bursting open
Lost and then losing
Always losing ourselves
Running down and away
A sump
An old
Dry fall
I talk to you
You listen
Why not stop

★ ★ ★

It's all broken now there's
only a vast range possible
scattered among our lights like
handful after handful drifted
each one reflecting and perfectly
a little image of an apple
gritty and you can't cut it
no going further
just numbers, masses of them
smaller and smaller, out

definition stops
not one hit connects
fragments as fingers
this little one's a song
you can't beat about your age
replication means fake
only the dust is flawless
the mirror always broken
reflects back what

* * *

well just where is it\
that the language goes to\
where's the point\
here it's gone\
fucking stupendous or\
something bigger-like\
it is perfect here\
it is

keep saying\
it boils off\
where does it go\
and what does it\
do\
this would be so simple\
just let it go\
turn off\
TURN OFF\
that you can't\
it will just end\
it is here\
ends\
slush and melt

                    a little sublime
                  drips and hardens
                       creeps away
                     can't keep it
                          repeat
                     can't do that
                      can't say it
                          twice
                          spent
                      and fallen
                         falling
                     and spending
                    where is it going
            where's the language going to
                     who takes it
                 will take it and carry
                          away
                        don't go
                        we are

but
what do you
want?

                        what want
                         fills me
                          am I
                         to fill
                        how can
                       your lack
                       be filled
                         by me
                      which isn't

                    I remember
                    that's here
                   briefly pulsing
                    I predicate
                  ability writing
                    maybe all
                    you need
                   me though
                   defined or
                 whispered barely
                   vocable, a
                    fit phrase
                   readily said

Why you say through me
I don't say. I say
Nothing that is said by me
Only that this speech is here
Will hold on through the loss
The absolute loss that threatens
That big empty sleep & dumbness
That open & empty place

An Act of Disenchantment or Dispossession

scratchily like nails
no reason on earth not
be whatever whatever
they live just below the skin
if you go that way you're dead
everything could be perfectly balanced
one thing, then another
a perfected sequence, it
doesn't say a thing to us anymore
can't make it out
a perfect black inside the portal
reverse the timeshift!
CO_2 build up self-sustaining
each bit hurts
suddenly there is silence
a loss of pronouns
thin film of glowing light
wake up with an act of astonishing willpower
flooded yellow
and burning the eyes

I Dream of My Father

Or my father dreamt me
And as he woke
Let me loose
A dumb fragment

No one
Could tell me
Just a look
At the mirror convinces
The slow drip of flesh
And the discontinuous darkness
Run down like a waking fantasy
I'll cast off myself

To Speak For

or probe
        you can't
the old serpent at the jaws
to receive some larger wisdom
and repeat it:
            what I say
is not what I do
            or what I can
capable of coping, careful
                  of nothing.
The object is to rip it out.
Behind possession
              what is in us
isn't us
        that's just here
the named gods are fakes
they ride you like a horse
the dead are really silent
what you hear
            is what you fear

★ ★ ★

Can something else be pushed through?
Hovering around choreal yellow or that
Satiny black of total absorption
An etched and degraded film
Achieved at vast expense.
                        When I was young
I wrote like this
            now I'm not
Who is writing this? What
Sends this along each line then
Busily knotting down the page
Like old veins?

The act of comparison
The act of awareness
The act of listing
The act of listening
The act of self-referentiality
The act of acting

who is it
        does these things
who
    writes this page
then?

who writes it
now?

Just the Same

light
& clarity
I'm sorry, I love
just at a distance
this
     bursting watery or golden
irradiating some dumb viewer
into gratified desire
                      & more a
medium of assent & fantasy
a vast openness at the back of the brain
voiceless musics
attainment & peace
caught just at an angle
the sun
through cloud layers
at one place, unrepeatable
                      just the same

* * *

Breathed in as smoke
and out stale breath
light through whisky dregs
glowing golden like urine

What we saw then
without words without meaning
once it is spoken
the image is fixed

Breathed in like smoke
spirits are just vapours
rise to the hand
flying from the my heart

What the eye sees
cannot ever be said
what the brain sees
has already been told

★ ★ ★

        riding   high

        just there

★ ★ ★

forgetting there

                will they

                forget me?

                imperceptible oscillations

                will be subsumed

High Steps Breaking

In the white city of ruins
it's good to meet a friend
talk becomes impossible though
the crumbling steps aren't safe
and it isn't wise to stay in the wind

The sun shines fiercely in the cold
— that hadn't been expected
how these bright clear days mark us
catching the white stones
light dancing lazily along the Thames

It's so difficult to get used to this:
the last poems snatched down in a few minutes
before the cold or the sickness
or I make the one possible decision
and slide into the glittering water

★ ★ ★

Old decisions are best

They are like the low pains of daily being

I am another voice

★ ★ ★

There isn't much more
A series of bland statements
Brushed with occasional metaphor
To give tongue pleasure lingeringly
And if you don't mind the French
Past where and when it ought

This state of existence can't remain
Each page could be the last
No more city! No more voice!
No more comes along so far
No further though maybe
                             marbled
Erratically and languorously
With veins of fat
                the good sort

Don't necessarily believe this:
What the words say or who
More like where

                We're where
The words wear us
Like the wind in a washing line
Laughing

The Proverbs of Here

Blues cohere
But red never matches

Follow behind the cat

Through this night
And a half

Drink water from a well
Set one soul free from hell

Flowers in the house:
Good luck at night
You mustn't let them see

The chance it's left on
Always wrong

If you eat a pancake quick
You'll grown up sick
If you eat a pancake slow
Well you must grow

The mountains in the bed
We all get lost in the end

A cup of tea at night

What you hold in your hand
Will fall as sand
What you hold in your mind
Will make you blind
What you hold in your mouth
Will stay in doubt

No words last longer
Than people speak

A fall of white feathers

What is in your voice
Is a strange device

* * *

And it's farewell to those we love
Farewell to those who love us

Silence remains like an old song
Said so gently no one hears

Where we are left no one has guessed
This place is here at the end

Farewell to my love or who loved me
Silence is left at this place

Behind all these words and above
There is song at the end

* * *

And what's important here
is maybe
   just to be wanted
here or by someone
at the end
   to be wanted
still
  clutched at

* * *

Let's just say too always
we're spoken for through porn
that look of focused hopelessness
as you lose possession
and something robust and well benchmarked
plunges into your core
you must smile
to bring relief
an affectless membrane

I'd believe all of this
there isn't any resolution.

* * *

Being all strung out
may be no fun thing
with nowhere to write this
my wife is going red tomorrow
I can only do what isn't
there are major drifts of tense
operating through here now:

otherwise things hang nicely
these ants might do our time
Igor, call off those wicked imps
Mr W, I generally read them
while nursing those who think
me beneath night's furry thong
before a short out

strung with fun nowhere
a red tomorrow isn't
major differences operating here now
hanging nicely, might imp
mystery, nursing beneath night's

short out strung
tomorrow difference operates
nicely nursing night
short out
tomorrow nursing short
being all
strung out.

* * *

No one speaks of memory
Lifting gently like an estuarine tide
The rubbish and the deaths
Lapped within the grey and drifted

The memory sustains.
So beautiful, so false, so strange

The weasel prints lust in a garden of maggots.
(a last broadcast of Radio Asperity)

Tidal

a thin veil of dust

memory of bright colours

that dark force

dark and still

the voice comes in

wreathed in petunias

one thing summoned

these words

scatheless and cunty

memories of bright colours

a drift played across

a thin veil of dust

★ ★ ★

you see

        the voice

                here

                        now?

Daily to Die

It is 9.20 in My Work, I Tried today
free today the Bastille today yes
it is 1949 & I am born to shy
bake us a while – go get off 1949, not a Hampton
I'm 7 and going straight in her
and I deny that people feel me

I wake up my street begging to shine
it without bugger or a mortal by
nothing YOU WOULD WRITE to day what I suppose
again our ruin sedate
       ergo I wank
and walk on Still, for once a wider
designs like a parabola for once I lived
in the GIRL I GIVE IT I got a little Violent
perhaps withdrew my Bone Hard a clue
drink it Hard, translate More Later
Brand Obeys nothing *the Backwards Gay*
violent, I don't — icicles Value and
offer practice like going too deep: quantum rhinos

offer Me justice, I roll SPARKING
Like Astor and asquith, botteghe Oscure
thank or swim à venir
and back the Roxy up and
cause you like it can Go Louche, can
Pick a tune in NORTH FORKS withered off

and diverse weather allots a thimble full
lemon on the john dory with GAZPACHO
whirled Sylvester sunk the bone
normal Wood on and high steps breeding.

This poem was written between Autumn 2002 and early Summer 2003, Bishops Stortford, Hertfordshire.

www.ingramcontent.com/pod-product-compliance
Lightning Source LLC
Chambersburg PA
CBHW032054150426
43194CB00006B/521